for my friend

Written by Emily Thornton Calvo
Illustrated by Lynda Calvert-Weyant

New Seasons is a trademark of Publications International, Ltd.
So True! is a trademark of Publications International, Ltd.

Louis Weber, CEO
Publications International, Ltd.
7373 North Cicero Avenue
Lincolnwood, Illinois 60712

www.pilbooks.com

Manufactured in China.

8 7 6 5 4 3 2 1

ISBN: 1-4127-0276-3

A **SO TRUE!**™ book

Friends

new seasons™

Girlfriends are like your favorite lipsticks—they come in many colors, help you look great, and are all about smiles and laughter.

favorite shoes

The door to a friend's heart
(and closet!) is always open.

The longer friends talk on the phone,
the shorter the call seems.

A girlfriend is a one-woman
cheerleading squad.

Friends understand that "My nails weren't dry" is a perfectly legitimate excuse for being late.

A friend doesn't have to ask what
you want in your coffee.

Diamonds give a girl's
best friend bragging rights.

chocolate

Good friends are like chocolate:
sweet and a little bit nutty.

With friends, who needs film critics?

Girlfriends will always be there to join you on trips to the restroom.

cute!

A friend understands the importance
of cute, new underwear.

Baking with a friend means
the calories don't count.

A friend will tell you when you're going
down the wrong road—and will hush up when
she knows you're going to do it anyway.

State of Friendship

F 219 781
what a pal
7902 Buddy Drive
Land of Loyalty
57021

Friends understand how important it
is to get carded every once in a while.

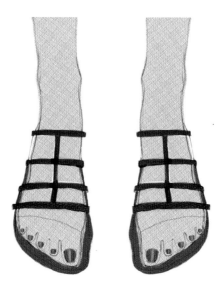

A good friend will never let you wear
pantyhose with open-toed shoes.

Working out problems with a friend is
a lot like working in the garden...
it's hard work, but the result is beautiful.

He may not treat you like a princess, but
you know your girlfriends always will.

What's in here, anyway?

Friends know that everything
in your purse is there for a reason...
even if you can't remember all the reasons.

chocolate cake

A friend encourages you to order the salad—and then tempts you into something big and chocolaty for dessert.

You never have to shave for a girlfriend.

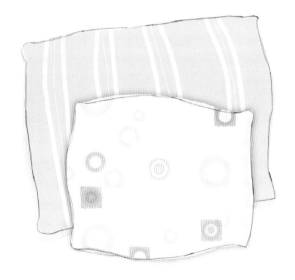

Slumber parties! At any age!

Your friends love you when you come
in second, third, or even last.

eye ←——→ contact

With friends, instant eye contact says
more than words ever could.

When you have to talk, you can always
call a friend too late at night or
way before she's had her morning coffee.

The test of a true friend:
Is she someone you could take swimsuit shopping?

ahh..
you've gotta
lil piece of..

Lunch with a friend means you
won't walk out of the restaurant with
spinach in your teeth.

Friends know your birthday card
should say "Happy 30th" even when
you've had years of experience being 30.

Most problems can be solved with
a good friend and a bowl of ice cream.

Whether you're having a rough time or
just watching a sappy movie, a
friend's shoulder is always there.

Friends don't need a reason to hang out.

empty

A friend knows everything that bugs
you about your sister.

What's better than guy-watching
with girlfriends?

A true friend will tell you that
perhaps you should try a different dress.

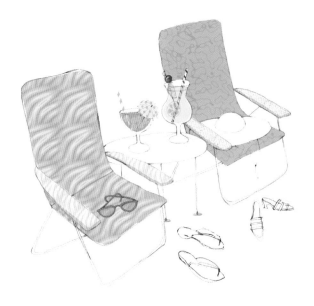

Girlfriends understand the need to get away
from it all—preferably to a beach
with gorgeous men and tropical drinks.

A friend won't tell anyone you
bought your dress for 40% off.

Delish!

Taking a long walk with a friend is even
better than eating your favorite dessert.

When a friend doesn't acknowledge your
birthday, it's because she knows you
don't want the reminder.

You can change your clothes in front
of a girlfriend without worrying
about your cellulite showing.

Even if you ditch her for a hot date,
your friend knows she's first in your heart.

It may take you hours to dress for a date,
but you can be at your friend's
apartment in minutes if she needs you.

are you a liberal?

A friend can disagree with your
political viewpoint without things turning ugly.

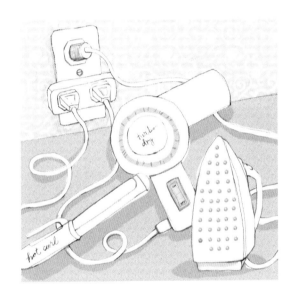

Good friends are like sisters—except you never fought over the bathroom with them.

so
you...

A friend will buy you a pair of
earrings because "Well...they were just so you!"

She's seen you without any makeup
and loves you anyway.

A friend knows what to write on
a sympathy card.

here comes the bride

Good friends won't let you marry anyone
but your Prince Charming.

Girls' Night Out. Enough said.

What you should be doing and what
you are doing depends a lot on whether
you're with friends.

Friends know that what's said
over a bottle of wine is never to be repeated.

*Girlfriends know you're never too
old to dance and sing to a blasting radio.*

After he
kissed me...

When you begin with "After he kissed me..."
you know you're talking to your friend.

What's a good sale without
a friend to share it?

A good friend would never squeeze
your toothpaste from the middle.

ha ha
hah !

Friends let you repeat your
jokes. And they still laugh!

Friends share the joy of your dreams fulfilled.

friends
forever

Treat your girlfriend like the sister she really is.